Enchanting
BALI & LOMBOK

DAVID BOWDEN

JOHN BEAUFOY PUBLISHING

Contents

Above left: Bali has a lively and colourful culture with an ancient dance tradition.

Above centre: Tanah Lot is one of Bali's most revered temples.

Above right: The food of Lombok is mostly spicy – chillies like those sold in Lombok's Sengkol Market provide a fiery quality to many dishes.

Opposite: Like Sanur, few locations on Bali are far from the mountainous interior.

Title page: The colourful entrance to the Gedong Kirtya Library and Museum in Singaraja on Bali.

Chapter 1: Island of the Gods

Of all the Asian islands, Bali is probably the one with the highest tourism profile and on the wishlist of most travellers to Asia. This paradise island is regularly voted as one of the world's favourite travel destinations and has long been characterized as one of the last paradises on Earth.

While Bali is part of the Indonesian nation and archipelago of some 18,300 islands, it is often perceived as a separate island state. Many travellers who venture to this part of Southeast Asia also include the neighbouring Gili Islands and Lombok Island in their travel itinerary.

While much, but not all, of Indonesia is predominantly Muslim (including Lombok and the Gili Islands), the people who live on Bali are mostly Hindu. With these differing faiths, the customs and cultures of Bali and Lombok are different and provide more reason to visit both islands.

Religion does, however, pervade all facets of life on both Bali and Lombok. Evidence of religious worship is found all over Bali, be it someone making a small offering to the gods, a temple, church or mosque or the full attendance at a major festival; all leading it being described as the Island of the Gods.

Left: Bali is a holiday island with many well-known resorts, such as the Rama Candidasa in Candi Dasa.

Opposite top: Lombok is also famous for its beaches. Putri Nyale in front of the Novotel Lombok Resort is the most picturesque in the Kuta area.

Opposite below: Hinduism forms an important part of daily life in Bali with most Balinese regularly making offerings to the gods.

Bali's major attractions are its seas, sun and surf but it also has many cultural attributes. Its temples, colourful festivals and dramatic landscape set it apart from most other islands in the region. The touristy areas are principally in the south and within a short drive of the new terminal facilities at Ngurah Rai International Airport (better known as Denpasar). While there are other resort and tourist areas on the island they are less visited and provide relief to those escaping the often crowded and most western of all Bali's locations, Kuta Beach.

Geography and Climate

Visitors to Bali are immediately impressed by the warm weather and magical landscapes from coral reefs, long sandy beaches and endless fields of swaying rice to towering volcanic peaks.

Both Bali and Lombok are small islands. Bali is 150 km (93 miles) at its longest point and Lombok 80 km (50 miles). Both lie just to the east of Java, Indonesia's most populous island. Bali is 5,632 km² (2,175 sq miles) in area while Lombok is 4,725 km² (1,824 sq miles). It's hard to miss the volcanic peaks of Bali and Lombok as several large mountains rise high above the lowlands. Mount Agung is Bali's highest peak at 3,142 m (10,308 ft). It's also the most revered mountain of all with important religious significance to most Balinese. Mount Rinjani at 3,726m (12,224 ft) is Lombok's tallest mountain.

The 35 km (22 miles) of the Lombok Strait that separates the two islands is one of the most important stretches of water known to biogeography. The strait delineates the imaginary Wallace Line named after British naturalist Alfred Russel Wallace. In 1859 Wallace identified this line as the boundary between the ecozones of animals with Asian and those with Australian origins (Bali with Asian origins and Lombok with Australian characteristics). Plants partly but not fully follow the Wallace Line as distinctly as the fauna. These field observations contributed to Wallace's greatest claim to fame in that he independently and in isolation postulated one of the most important theories known to science: the theory of evolution through natural selection attributed to Charles Darwin.

Being equatorial (8° S of the Equator), Bali experiences high temperatures and rainfall. The temperature remains constantly warm (an average of 26°C/79°F) for most of the year in the lowlands. Coastal temperatures are ameliorated by sea breezes and the mountains can be several degrees cooler than the lowlands. The monsoon (the seasonal reversal of tropical winds followed by heavy downfalls of rain) from October to March is accompanied by high humidity and short, sharp rainfalls in the afternoon.

As it is mostly an agrarian society, water is very important on Bali and Lombok. A water management or irrigation system of canals and weirs, called *subak*, dates back to the ninth century and is so important to every facet of Balinese life that UNESCO has recognized it as a World Heritage Site (there are five locations covering 19,500 ha / 47,000 acres). In one of the world's first and most permanent forms of ecological sustainability, water flows through temples that are under the control of priests through to rice fields. Rice is seen as a gift of god and this cooperative social system of *subak* has shaped the Balinese landscape. As forests and mountains protect the source of most water they are also included in the management of Bali's 1,200 water collectives.

Opposite: Both Bali and Lombok are volcanic islands fringed by long stretches of sandy beaches. Here Mount Agung is seen in the distance from Benoa.

Right: These rice terraces near Ubud are part of an ancient water management system called 'subak', recognized by UNESCO as a World Heritage Site.

History

Throughout their history, both Bali and Lombok have been influenced by empires in nearby Java and Sumbawa. Trade with their neighbours dates back over 2,000 years and evidence suggests that Buddhism and Hinduism originating from the Indian subcontinent have been practised on Bali for centuries.

Bali and Lombok were, up until the 19th century, divided into kingdoms ruled over by rajas. On occasions these kingdoms extended over both islands. Almost 700 years ago Bali was conquered and colonized by Gajah Mada who led the Hindu Majapahit Kingdom of East Java. By 1515 Islam dominated Java and Hindu believers fled to Bali. Historians are unclear as to how Bali remained Hindu when neighbouring Java and Lombok converted to Islam.

Trade with China is thought to have started two millennia ago; Bali first became known to Europe when Dutch explorers visited at the end of the 15th century. Europeans initially came to the region to trade with the neighbouring Maluka Islands (formerly the Moluccas) or 'spice islands' and later the Dutch East Indies Company introduced colonial rule to both Bali and Lombok. European empire building reached its peak in the region in the 19th century.

Historical evidence remains patchy at the ancient sites on both islands. One of the oldest of these is Pura Maospahit in Bali's capital, Denpasar. Made entirely from brick, the oldest section of this temple is thought to have originated from the Majapahit Kingdom of East Java in the 14th century, though what visitors see today is a temple constructed from both original and replacement bricks because much of it was destroyed by an earthquake in 1917. This rarely visited temple is remarkable for its simplicity and lack of ornamentation. There are some impressive ancient representations here of the Hindu gods of Yama, Indra and Sankara.

Above: Denpasar's Pura Maospahit is one of the oldest in Bali with understated carvings of Hindu gods, such as Indra.

Opposite below: The revered Water Palace at Tirtagangga: a maze of pools and fountains, in recognition of the importance of water to the Balinese.

Close by, on the northern side of Puputan Square in the centre of Denpasar, a large statue stands as a memorial to the local Badung people who committed suicide or were shot in 1906 at the hands of Dutch forces. The Raja of Badung decided that he and his people should die rather than be ruled over by the Dutch. Their efforts were in vain as Dutch authority was enforced with a policy designed to uphold traditional Balinese values that still enabled the colonial masters to run a lucrative colony. Independence for the whole of Indonesia from the colonial Dutch was finally attained in 1949.

In the town of Mengwi, just to the north of Denpasar, the state temple of Pura Taman Ayun was built in 1634 on the orders of Raja I Gusti Agung Anom as the focus of his powerful dynasty, which remained in power for the next 250 years. The temple is one of the most important historical structures from this era and is a popular tourist attraction.

By the late 19th century, most of the kingdoms in south Bali lost their independence. One of the last signs of the rajas is the Water Palace at Tirtagangga on the east coast near Amlapura that was completed in 1947.

The People

There are 3.3 million residents on Bali and 3.2 million on Lombok. However, during the peak months of July to September, in December, January, Chinese New Year and the end of the Muslim fasting month of Ramadan, these numbers swell by another three million due to the annual influx of tourists.

Being predominantly Hindu (93%), Bali stands out as the most populous Hindu nation in the world. Balinese Hinduism differs from Indian Hinduism in that it is a blend of practices and theories borrowed from both Buddhism and traditional Hinduism. Hindu temples are the most obvious signs of the religion – there are tens of thousands of temples over the island where deities are honoured – but there are many others, such as the ubiquitous offerings (*banten*) to the gods, ancestors and demons; the household shrines and the numerous festivals.

Religion permeates all levels of Balinese society and the rituals of daily life. Offerings can be seen at temples, on the beach, in front of a shop or on the footpath at the entrance to a restaurant. These are used to bar the entry of demonic forces, to safeguard the people or the business, in memory of ancestors or as a prayer for wealth or fertility. As they are offerings to higher beings they must be ornate and elaborate and thus require a great deal of time and effort, usually on the part of women.

Left: *Colourful flowers are offered by Hindus to their gods.*

Above: *Some Balinese, like this man from Medewi, still wear traditional clothes.*

These offerings may be in the form of tiny packets called *canang* which are palm leaves containing flowers and betel as a token of hospitality. Others are presented to resident gods after food has been prepared and before it is eaten by the family. Offerings are colourful and come in many different shapes and forms depending on the celebration.

Above: *Religious festivals and processions like this one in Ubud occur in Bali on an almost daily basis.*

Right: *Preparing 'canang' is either done in the home or more commonly these days by market traders for sale to devotees.*

Balinese society is very tolerant of other religions and this is no more evident than in Puja Mandala in southern Bali near Nusa Dua where five different religious buildings stand side by side: a Buddhist and a Hindu temple, a Catholic and a Protestant church and an Islamic mosque. Despite only a small percentage of Balinese being Muslim there are some 2,000 mosques.

Also in the north of Bali, there are a few Chinese temples such as Ling Gwan Kiong Temple located along the beachfront at Singaraja near several original Dutch colonial buildings which have been modified to make their origins almost unrecognizable.

Things are markedly different on Lombok as the Sasak people are Muslim and only three per cent of the islanders are Hindu. While mosques are common throughout the island, religious activities are less evident than on Bali although the islanders are devout worshippers. This also means that the lively bars and clubs of Bali are almost non-existent on Lombok and then, mostly restricted to Senggigi.

Below: This Buddhist temple in Bali co-exists next to four other places of worship all for different religions.

Opposite: A mosque in the farming village of Dasan Tapen in the Gerung district; one of many seen on Lombok.

Food

Bali is well and truly on the tourist trail and this means comfort food from around the globe is widely available. Whether it's tacos, risotto, burgers, fries, pizza or banana pancakes, visitors can be assured of getting it somewhere.

For those who travel to discover the local culture that hosts them, there is also a vibrant local culinary scene on both Bali and Lombok. Because of the differing religions on these islands, the food is distinctive with the main distinction being that the Lombok Muslims do not eat pork whereas one of the most prized Balinese dishes is *babi guling* (spit-roasted pork). It is sold in many restaurants, such as *Ibu Oka* (Ubud), *Warung Dobil* (Nusa Dua) and *Bumbu Bali* (Benoa).

Rice (called *nasi*) is the staple food grown all over both islands. While several varieties are grown, it is mostly polished and served white as an accompaniment at most meals, with a favourite dish being *nasi goreng* (fried rice). While the latter is Chinese in origin, it is a way for Balinese homemakers to recycle rice from a previous meal. Dishes are usually delicately spiced with chilli, ginger, garlic, lemongrass, soy sauce and turmeric. Fresh seafood (mostly in coastal villages), chicken, beef and pork provide the protein in Balinese diets.

Fruit is commonly sold in markets and available all over the islands. Some of the more unusual Asian fruits include *salak* (snake fruit), durian (the 'king of fruits' that smells unpleasant but is tasty) and jackfruit (known as *cempedak*

Above right: Ibu Oka' in Ubud is one of Bali's most famous 'babi guling' (spit-roasted pork) restaurants.

Right: Bali's climate encourages the vigorous growth of many fruits, such as (clockwise from top left) durian, chillies, jackfruit and snake fruit.

on Bali). Visit markets like those in Ubud (Bali) and Sengkol (Lombok) to appreciate how many islanders shop, best seen from 6 to 8 a.m.

Food is served in a wide range of places from rustic roadside *warungs* (hawker stalls) to iconic and legendary beachside or *padi* field-sited restaurants. Common and inexpensive *warung* dishes include *nasi campur* (vegetable, meat and fish dishes accompanied by rice and usually selected from a wide variety on offer) and *bakso ayam* (meatballs and chicken soup).

Pepesan ikan is a local Balinese speciality of fish steamed in banana leaves. *Betutu bebek* (smoked duck) is slow-cooked in an earthen oven and normally ordered well in advance as all true 'slow food' should be. The name is misleading as it is actually steamed within the bark of the betel nut palm. Other local dishes include *sate lilit* (seafood satay) and *urap jaggung* (sweet corn and coconut). *Kambing merkuah* (lamb stew) is popular on Lombok. *Gado-gado* (raw vegetable, spicy peanut sauce and sticky rice) is a popular Indonesian dish served in both Bali and Lombok.

It is now fashionable for resorts to offer cooking classes to their guests. Bali's pioneer and most authentic is *Bumbu Bali Restaurant and Cooking School* in Tanjung Benoa. Lessons start with a visit to the markets followed by hands-on lessons in a professional kitchen and then the opportunity to enjoy the dishes prepared.

Various locally produced beverages add to the Balinese dining experience. *Bintang* is the most common brand of beer and *Hatten Wines* made from grapes grown near Lovina are available in all tourist areas. Bali is one of the 'new latitude' countries producing wines in the New World.

The food served on Lombok is mostly *halal* as it is prepared according to Islamic laws. Rice is the staple and accompanied by spicy dishes, such as vegetables, seafood and meats (no pork). Beer is available especially in the tourist areas.

Top: 'Ikan bakar' (grilled fish) is a dish common to both Bali and Lombok.

Above: 'Nasi goreng' (fried rice) is usually served with a fried egg-and-prawn cracker.

Unique Habitats

While Bali and Lombok are equatorial islands a variety of habitats and ecosystems can be found here. Habitats range from coral reefs, sandy beaches, mangroves, agricultural land, rainforests, montane forests and savannah. The generally lush vegetation results from the combination of high temperatures, rainfall and humidity.

Both islands are encircled by coral reefs and although many have been damaged and over-exploited, others thrive and appeal to scuba divers and snorkellers. The best diving is off northern Bali and around the Gili Islands but dive operators are generally based in the south around Sanur and Benoa where there are most facilities. Divers can see parrotfish, angelfish and butterflyfish, barracuda, tuna and possibly White-tipped Reef Sharks.

Sandy beaches line the foreshore of most parts of the islands although mangroves are evident in some locations. These beaches can be golden yellow, white or black depending on the geological source of the parent material with black sand beaches being volcanic in origin. The popular beaches are best described as landscaped with little natural vegetation remaining. Less developed beaches tend to have overhanging vegetation. Seaweed is harvested from many of the beaches.

Wetlands, in particular mangroves, are located along some coastlines. These also extend inland and line some of the riverbanks of coastal rivers. They are important breeding grounds for fish and crustaceans. Mangroves can be found around Kuta in southern Lombok and Benoa in Bali. In the Benoa mangroves it is not unusual to see religious references, such as *tedung* (golden Hindu umbrellas), amongst the mangroves.

Although many parts of Bali have been converted to agricultural land, they are still an important habitat for some animals, especially birds. *Padi* fields in particular are important for the survival of bird species, such as the Watercock, Cinnamon Bittern, Ruddy-breasted Crack and Plumed, Cattle and Little Egrets. Bali's rice terraces have been in existence for many hundreds of years and are well-established habitats. Landscaped gardens in many of the resorts are quite extensive and now home to some animals.

Opposite: Not all beaches are golden in colour; some like this one just north of Sengiggi on Lombok are black.

Right: Mangroves grow along some shorelines, such as this stand on Lombok's Kuta Beach.

Right: Mountain streams and lush rainforests are common in Bali's interior.

Opposite top left: Flowering epiphytic orchids grow on the branches of many trees within rainforests.

Opposite top right: Giant tree ferns thrive in the cooler altitudes of the mountains.

Opposite below: Bamboo thickets grow in Bali's moist humid climate.

Bali's climate of high rainfall and high temperatures is perfect for rainforests to thrive. However, Bali is a highly modified and altered environment and experts estimate that the primary forest that once covered much of the island now only accounts for about 20%, mostly found in the mountainous peaks in the centre of the island.

Forests in the foothills of Bali's second highest peak, Mount Batukaru (2,276 m/7,467 ft), just south of Pupuan in the centre of the island, support many features of the rainforest from buttress roots to lianas, tree ferns, orchids, bird's nest ferns and bamboo groves with mosses and fungus in the higher altitudes. These forests are also home to the Barking Deer, Pangolin (ant-eater), Porcupine, Palm Civet, Reticulated Python and Leopard Cat. The Mountain Chorus Frog, one of the world's smallest, lives here as does the Atlas Moth, one of the world's largest. Guides from the Sarinbuana Trekking Guide Association lead walks into the Batukaru Rainforest.

On the more exposed slopes of the mountain peaks, there is virtually no vegetation as the volcanic rocks present a harsh environment unsuitable for plant growth.

The volcanic peaks and high rainfall ensure that there is an abundance of water channelled down the many rivers that flow from the mountains to the sea. Rocky streams radiate from the volcanic peaks in the centre of the island, the longest of which is the Ayung River at 75 km (47 miles).

Flora

While not every part of Bali and Lombok is covered in lush vegetation, the equatorial climate ensures that many parts are. Plant growth is affected by the dry season (from April to October), soil conditions and the rain shadow effect from the towering volcanic peaks.

Opposite top: Orchids grow in many ecosystems all over both islands.

The rain shadow effect is caused when air that is forced over a mountain deposits its moisture on the windward side, leaving the leeside dry. Bali is the world's seventh most important plant biome: an estimated 30,000 plant species grow here. One of the most commonly seen flowers is the purple flourish of the blooms of the Punyan Tangi Tangi tree that have religious significance as they are used by the Balinese to purify an area from a 'bad past'.

The landscaped tropical gardens found in most of the large resorts are also impressive. Species with colourful flowers, variegated leaves and fascinating fruits have been planted to enliven the gardens and to encourage animal life, especially birds, to visit. However, many of these flowers

Above: Brightly-coloured heliconia flowers adorn most landscaped gardens.

Right: Waterlilies of various colours can be seen growing in ornamental ponds.

are not native to Bali or even the region but thrive in the lush climatic conditions.

Desert Rose has a colourful pink flower and originates from Africa and Arabia. Other flowering plants that typically appear in landscaped designs are heliconias, gingers, frangipani and waterlilies.

Beautiful lotus flowers flourish in ponds all over Bali. This pink, aquatic perennial flower is native to tropical Asia. From its underwater roots, a gracious flower rises up to be one of the most beautiful sights imaginable; revered by Hinduism and other religions. As well as being admired for its intrinsic beauty, it is an economically valuable plant as parts of it are eaten and others are used to wrap food for cooking or in markets to wrap produce. Pura Saraswati and the appropriately named *Lotus Café* nearby in the main street of Ubud are excellent locations to see lotus flowers.

Left: While ginger is important for cooking, the flowers also make many gardens more colourful.

Above: Flashes of the abundant purple flowers of the Punyan Tangi Tangi tree are seen all over Bali.

Fauna

In 1859 naturalist Alfred Russel Wallace (see page 6) discovered that the mammals found on Bali and Lombok were different apart from a few bats and the Long-tailed Macaque (or Crab-eating Macaque) which are found on both Bali and Lombok.

Macaques can be seen in many environments from rainforest to beaches. They live in groups of 20 or more including many young. They are omnivores with plants comprising the bulk of their diet but, despite the name, eat very few crabs. They have become accustomed to humans and are pests in many locations. Signs indicating the need to be careful of belongings, such as sunglasses, are common all over the island. Monkeys have special status in Hinduism and many inhabit temples like Pura Luhur Uluwatu and forests in Sangeh and Ubud.

Above: *Monkeys are the most commonly seen animals on Bali especially around temples.*

Below: *Dolphins live in the waters surrounding both islands.*

Dolphins are common in Bali's waters making dolphin watching one of Lovina's main attractions. Conservationists aren't as enthusiastic about the dolphin 'chasing' as are most tourists but it does provide an opportunity to get close to Spinner and Bottlenose Dolphins.

Turtles were once abundant off Bali but poaching and fishing-net kills have taken their toll. Green Turtles especially are prized for their meat, despite being protected, and turtle eggs are stolen from the beaches.

Some 300 bird species (both Oriental and Australasian) have been identified on Bali with Rothschild's Myna (Jalak Bali) being endemic and endangered.

Rice terraces and *padi* fields support many bird species, among them Cattle Egrets that have a symbiotic relationship with their namesakes: egrets consume ticks on the cattle while cattle disturb the soil and expose insects to the waiting beaks of egrets. Thousands of egrets return to roost each evening in the village of Petulu near Ubud. In the morning, they disperse en masse to feed throughout the island.

The extensive landscaped gardens of the resorts provide a refuge for reptiles, insects and butterflies. Birds like the Spotted Dove, sunbirds, spiderhunters, bulbuls, flowerpeckers and Wren-Warblers are common.

Left: Cattle Egrets with honey-coloured breeding plumage are one of the most commonly seen birds.

Top: Butterflies, such as this Peacock Pansy, provide colour to the forests of both islands.

Above: Rothschild's Myna, known locally as Jalak Bali.

Land and Resources

Volcanic peaks in Bali's north and east dominate the skyline. Their foothills radiate down to the lowlands in the south around Denpasar and Singaraja in the north. Lombok is not dissimilar in that Mount Rinjani in the north rises up to the clouds while two-thirds of the island to the south is flat.

Below and opposite top left: Manual and animal labour is common on both islands.

While there are several large urban areas on both islands, many locals live in small, close-knit villages with temples at their core.

Tourism is the largest contributor to the Balinese economy but most of the locals are engaged in agricultural activity of which rice production is the most common. Other farm crops include vegetables, fruit, cacao, grapes and coffee while seaweed is harvested along the coast. Balinese are also employed in the fishing industry or as artisans producing a vast array of handicrafts from wood carving to art, silverware, *batik* and household furniture.

Rice production is aided by the village *subak* (see page 7). In many parts of Bali rice is grown within a system of intricate terraces. Before planting, the land is ploughed

using buffalo or tractors. Natural fertilizers and compost enrich the soil. Young plants are normally transplanted from a nursery plot, then nurtured until they are harvested 200 days later. At least two crops overlap each other and when they are fully ripened, they are harvested by hand, then threshed and winnowed to remove all but the rice grains. These are stored and used as required.

Fishing provides many Balinese with a valuable source of protein. This is obtained from aquaculture farms or wild-catch fishing by fleets of boats around Bali and Lombok. One of the most visible fleets is based in Kedonganan fishing village along the popular Jimbaran beachfront.

Left: Seaweed is an important cash crop. Carrageenan contained in the seaweed is used as a gelling, thickening and stabilizing agent in food production and cosmetics.

Above right: Grapes are grown in northern Bali and used to produce wine as well as for consumption as a fruit.

Adventures and Lifestyle

B ali has a lot to offer tourists both on the land and in the surrounding waters. While many tourists simply come to relax, others are attracted to cultural encounters, adventurous activities, shopping and the hectic nightlife in some of the southern beach destinations.

Above: *Swift-flowing rivers in the mountainous regions of Bali attract whitewater-rafting enthusiasts.*

Opposite: *Surfers from around the globe come to surf breaks like those off Gili Trawangan.*

Watersport activities line Bali's busy resort beaches. Learn-to-surf classes are popular along Kuta Beach and while diehard surfers prefer Echo Beach in Canggu to the north, the waves rolling in on the Kuta reef still make it a hot surfing destination. The dry season with offshore winds from March to November provide the best surfing conditions. Distinctive red and yellow surf flags are used on the main beaches and most are patrolled by lifesavers.

Shallow waters within the reefs surrounding Bali are safe for snorkelling too, although many reefs have been seriously denuded over the years. Scuba diving is best off the north coast and the Gili Islands. Many accredited dive operators are located along the main beach of Gili Trawangan and Bali's best dive sites are to be found off Amed, Candi Dasa and Deer Island (Pulau Menjangan).

With so many natural and cultural assets, there appears little need for themed attractions. However, Waterbom Bali is an exciting 3.8-ha (9½-acre) water-themed park with 20 slides and glides to entertain visitors of all ages. Located in landscaped tropical gardens in Kuta, Waterbom offers a pleasant respite from the beach.

Whitewater rafting along forest-lined rivers is one of the more adrenalin-charged activities offered on Bali. Several operators actively promote their tour packages on one of several wild rivers in the hinterland mostly around Ubud at Sayan on the Ayung River. Class II and III rapids add to the excitement through the Ayung Gorge especially after heavy rainfalls (the river is more docile from June to September).

Dolphin watching is popular in the north of Bali. Boatmen take visitors out onto the waters of the Bali Sea between 6 and 8 a.m. each morning to see Spinner and Bottlenose Dolphins when they are most active.

Timbis is a 1-km (1,100-yard) long ridgeline on the extreme southern tip of Bali, jutting out into the Indian Ocean. During the dry season (April to November) paraglider pilots from around the world flock to this spot to enjoy the easy flying conditions and the million dollar views out to sea, over Hindu temples and fishing villages and back up into Bali's volcanoes. The steady sea breeze at this time of year allows pilots to fly for hours, gliding to and fro along the generous ridgeline. Tandem flights for beginners are available.

Mountain climbing on both Bali and Lombok is available for those who want to make short sunrise climbs or more serious undertakings of several days to the lakes within active volcanic craters. Batur is Bali's most climbed peak while Rinjani challenges climbers on Lombok.

For something less active, health and spa resorts are growing in numbers and several yoga retreats cater to those visitors who want to get closer to Bali's spiritual core. Retreats, especially those in Ubud, tend to favour tranquil locations offering views of peaceful rice fields, majestic gorges, pristine forests or distant mountains.

Shopping for Indonesian antiques, tribal artefacts, surfwear, designer label fashions and home décor products (some visitors will load a container to ship back home) is an essential activity for many visitors. Arts and craft villages line most roads radiating out from Ubud and include *mas* (wood carvings), *batubulan/singakerta* (stone carvings), *batuan* (paintings) and *celuk* (silverware).

Opposite top: Dolphin watching off Lovina Beach is one of the north's 'must-do' activities.

Opposite below: The seventh hole of Nirwana Bali Golf Club is one of the world's most acclaimed, challenging and picturesque.

Above: Tandem paragliding over the coastline of southern Bali caters to the adventurous.

Chapter 2: Southern and Eastern Bali

Most tourists arrive and stay in the tourist areas in Bali's south. Kuta Beach is Bali's best known and one of the world's most famous beaches. Inland, Ubud also has a wide range of facilities for visitors in a more tranquil setting.

Kuta and Denpasar

Denpasar is the capital of Bali but most people come to bask on Bali's legendary beaches and soak up the sunshine at nearby Kuta. Only a few venture into bustling Denpasar. For those who do, there are several attractions that will appeal including historic buildings, temples, the museum and markets. Kuta is very international in all that it offers from world cuisines to clothing brands. A whole host of activities are available from surfing, beachside massage, bungy jumping, the Waterbom theme park, shopping, dining and generally having a good time.

Above right, above centre and right: *While Denpasar is home to 800,000 Balinese and fellow Indonesians, Kuta Beach is markedly different with a United Nations of foreign tourists attracted to the frenetic pace and party atmosphere. Kuta has the best beach on Bali and this means many people want to be here – tourists want to enjoy and experience the beach and all that it offers and many locals take the opportunity to provide services of every description to them. Seemingly every local is selling something.*

Above: Pasar Badung (Badung Market) is a sprawling and enclosed market located beside the Badung River in central Denpasar. This traditional three-storey space is brimming with merchandise that has special appeal to local shoppers who flock here. Markets provide a fascinating cultural experience especially for those new to Asia and many will be observers more than active shoppers although there are plenty of things to buy. Fresh produce is sold at the entrance and on the ground floor while textiles, such as 'batik', are available on the third floor. Bargaining is part of the retail theatre and is expected.

Right: Puputan Square is a peaceful parkland fronting the Bali Museum. The grounds of the museum, complete with traditional courtyards, provide an excellent introduction to Balinese architecture as they incorporate both palace and temple features. There is a reasonable collection of Balinese artefacts including theatrical masks, musical instruments, sculptures, textiles, paintings and archaeological remains.

Below right: The Pura Maospahit temple dating from the 14th century is an essential stop for those interested in Balinese culture. Located on Jalan Sutomo, just north of Badung Market, this Hindu temple is rarely visited by tourists. While it is not grand in scale, the brick temples and representations of various Hindu gods are intriguing.

Above: Several resorts face the golden sands of Bali's beaches, however, for many tourists, the resort pool will be as close as they come to enjoying all that Kuta Beach has to offer. Resorts, such as the Mercure Kuta Beach Bali (pictured) and the Hotel Pullman Bali Legian Nirwana, offer a comprehensive range of facilities. Both properties have commanding views over the beaches of Kuta and Legian.

Left: Kuta is also known as party central and from dusk until well into the early morning, the narrow congested streets are crammed with holidaymakers enjoying the brash and bold bars, energetic clubs and restaurants serving local and global cuisines. Hard Rock Café within Hard Rock Hotel is the most established and famous nightspot overlooking Kuta Beach.

Legian to Seminyak

The beaches on the west coast of the southern part of Bali continue northwards from Kuta to Legian and Seminyak. It is a continuous strip without any dramatic geographical change but the atmosphere becomes a little more sophisticated and quieter the further the distance from Kuta. The main retail action here is focussed on Jalan Seminyak which offers upmarket boutiques, restaurants, clubs and bars. Other high profile outlets are located immediately overlooking the beach. Several of these have become iconic establishments on the must-visit list of discerning travellers.

Above: Canggu beach is especially popular with surfers who are catered for by the surfing schools that operate here. Designated surfing areas are distinguishable by bright red and yellow flags but generally the waves rolling in off the reef ensure safe swimming conditions in the shallows. Boardriders head further offshore to make the most of the waves breaking on the reef.

Left: Cool beachside bars, cafés and clubs, independent and iconic restaurants, trendy boutiques and exclusive accommodation including many small and exclusive villas dominate the eight-kilometre (five-mile) long stretch of sandy beach from Kuta to Canggu just north of Seminyak.

This page: Many who come to Legian and Seminyak have made a conscious decision to escape the hustle and bustle of Kuta. Catering for them are several landmark resorts in the area including the MGallery Royal Beach Seminyak Bali (pictured), The Legian, the Anantara Seminyak Resort and Spa, the W Retreat and Spa, The Oberoi and The Semara. Guests are treated to extensive resort facilities including landscaped pools and rejuvenative spas.

The South – Nusa Dua, Benoa, Uluwatu and Jimbaran

The southern part of Bali includes the land south of the airport and takes in the popular tourist areas of Nusa Dua, Benoa and Jimbaran. Chic boutiques, spas and restaurants catering to discerning international travellers who stay at leading resorts, such as Ayana, Four Seasons and the Intercontinental, are located at the southern end of the bay below the airport. The pace of life is more relaxed than Kuta with limited nightlife apart from dining on the beach.

These pages: The first part of Bali that arriving passengers see from their aircraft window is Jimbaran located immediately to the south of the airport. The long sweeping bay is home to several resorts, an atmospheric fish market and a colourful fishing village. The beachfront restaurants along Jimbaran Bay are a popular place to enjoy fresh barbecued seafood, evening sunsets and the sight of planes coming into land.

Unlike many other parts of Bali, the parent rock in the south is limestone and not volcanic in origin. Officially known as Bukit Badung (or Badung Hill), the land rises gently from the coast to offer commanding views. The soil is impoverished and supports scrubby plants resembling the savannah found in Bali Barat National Park. Access is limited in the extreme south due to the vertical limestone cliffs. However, it is these cliffs that attract paraglider pilots during the dry season from April to November. Weather conditions are perfect for soaring along the coast.

Above right: While the steep cliff face along the extreme southern coastline, generally referred to as Uluwatu, has seen some resort development in recent years, it is still a difficult area to access with just a few remote but popular surfing beaches.

Centre: Benoa is a busy port and home to fishing vessels as well as boats that ferry tourists to neighbouring islands and reefs.

Right: Each day, the deep-blue painted boats of the fishing fleet head out to sea and return to Kedonganan fishing village along the Jimbaran beachfront near the fish market. Fishermen can be seen at other times repairing nets or maintaining their boats.

Above: Close proximity to the airport and the establishment of the purpose-built deluxe resort development of Nusa Dua (pictured) ensure that tourism blossoms around Bali's southeast corner and adjoining Benoa. Other international resorts include Novotel, Four Seasons, Nikko, Conrad, Westin, St. Regis, Grand Hyatt, Meli and Ibis.

Left: The Novotel Bali Nusa Dua Hotel and Residences is typical of most resorts in Nusa Dua in being close to the Convention Centre and the golf courses, and in providing deluxe accommodation amongst spacious, tropical landscaping. Its sister property, the Novotel Benoa Bali, is situated immediately on the golden sands of the tranquil Benoa Beach with dramatic views of Bali's volcanic peaks on the horizon. Novotel Benoa has various dining options and a tranquil spa featuring Balinese treatments.

Above: The road extends southward from Nusa Dua but peters out beyond the massive Mulia Resort and the Nikko Bali Resort and Spa. The former is located along the near-deserted Geger Beach that was once home to many seaweed farmers.

Right: The Pura Geger Temple is located on a headland that offers wonderful coastal views both north and south. The headland is popular with surfers who come here to work out where the best waves are.

Right: Bali has several iconic bars that have become tourist destinations in their own right amongst design-conscious travellers. One of them is the Rock Bar within the Ayana Resort and Spa Bali which is legendary for its geology rather than its music. This is one of Bali's best sunset bars perched on the rocks, below limestone cliffs and just above crashing waves. Live music, creative cocktails and an open-air setting create a magical experience.

Below: Beaches for seaweed harvesting, such as Pandawa, have a reputation as 'lost' or 'newly found' since they gained popularity with surfers who come for the budget accommodation, relaxed atmosphere and the good waves rolling in over the reef.

Sanur

Sanur on the eastern side of southern Bali has been settled since ancient times and was one of the first areas to be affected by tourism. Europeans originally made contact here in the mid 19th century and invading Dutch forces landed here in 1906. Celebrities and artists like Walter Spies arrived in the 1930s and others like Australian artist Donald Friend followed in the ensuing decades. The only reminder of this is Museum Le Mayeur, the former home and gallery of a Belgium artist who lived here for 60 years.

Opposite page: Today, Sanur attracts more sedate holidaymakers than Kuta who place less emphasis on active nocturnal pursuits. Jalan Danau Tambungan takes a long sweeping curve just back from the beachfront and is lined with restaurants, cafés, bars and boutiques. The Bali Hyatt is located in mature tropical gardens at the southern end of the beach.

Below: Permanent, open-air, beachside markets are common along Bali's main beaches with the one at the northern end of Sanur being popular for its local handicrafts, colourful beach attire and watersports equipment.

Below: Many visitors to Sanur are returnees who like the leisurely pace of life, its lesser commercialism and the opportunity to enjoy a massage beneath a shaded tree on the beach. Balinese massage is influenced by traditional medicines from India, China and parts of Southeast Asia. It's available all over the island from beachside locations to luxurious resort spas.

Ubud

About an hour's drive north of Denpasar, Ubud oozes with climatic and cultural cool. While only 200 m (656 ft) above sea level, the climate is decidedly cooler than the lowlands. There are actually 14 villages centred on Ubud and the district has long been known as Bali's arts and cultural centre. Ubud itself is brimming with trendy cafés, galleries, boutiques and legendary designer resorts.

Opposite: Most of Ubud's resorts are scattered throughout the district and blend into their surroundings so that they have a timeless feel, although may be newly built. Many have become destination properties that attract well-heeled guests seeking solitude and luxury in atmospheric locations. Alila Ubud Resort is perched in the rainforest high above the Ayung River near Payangan Village. Guests seek inspiration from the natural surroundings, participate in yoga sessions and laze around a carefully landscaped pool.

Right: Some resorts are located within rice-farming communities and are surrounded by swaying rice fields. The Chedi Club at Tanah Gajah nestles in the culturally-rich hills of the former estate of one of Indonesia's most esteemed art collectors. Guests enjoy its reviving qualities, serenity, views off to Bali's volcanic peaks and unparallelled luxury.

Below right: While Tegallalang rice terraces have become a little touristy these days, they are still well worth visiting. There are other rice terraces in the district most of which practise the water management called 'subak' (see page 7), such as Tabanan, Jatiluwih, Seririt Menduk and Sayan. Many terraces were cut into steeply sloping hillsides centuries ago to help retain water which is essential for growing the staple crop of rice.

Below and right: *Ubud Market is popular especially with day trippers who tend to end up here because this is a favourite drop-off location with tour guides. It has just been upgraded and sprawls over two floors but is crowded at midday when the tour buses arrive. There's no shortage of handicrafts and locally-made souvenirs.*

Above: *There are many craft villages around Ubud. While some artisans practise traditional crafts, such as silver jewellery making, many of the products are what may be considered 'export' crafts – those for foreigners and the overseas trade.*

This page: Ubud is also home to several popular tourist attractions including Taman Burung (Bali Bird Park), Rimba Reptil (Bali Reptile Park), Bali Zoo and Monkey Forest. Over 250 species are housed in the bird park while the zoo is home to 350 exotic and indigenous animals including African Lions and the colourful Eclectus Parrot (above). A new botanic garden located in a valley at Kutuh Kaja provides an excellent opportunity to appreciate some of Bali's unique flora.

East Coast

Bali's east coast is mostly a narrow strip of land gripping the coastline then rising gently inland to the peaks of two volcanoes that tower over the surrounding farms. These are Mount Seraya (1,238 m/4,062 ft) and Mount Agung (Bali's holiest mountain) at 3,142 m (10,308 ft) . It's as if the main volcanic peaks extend as one from the east coast into the northeastern interior. Roads cling to the coast and skirt around the base of Mount Seraya to provide access to several remote beach hideaways around Amed and Jemuluk.

Diving is what lures most people here, in particular the chance to explore the World War II wreck of the United States *Liberty* off Tulamben.

Below: *The best remnants of an ancient court of the Balinese kingdoms are at Taman Gili in Klungkung. Commercial activities now dominate this town with its local market and horse-drawn carts providing some interest for tourists.*

This page: Tourism infrastructure becomes less developed on the extreme northeastern coast. The centre for resorts, restaurants and bars is Candi Dasa just north of the Lombok ferry terminal of Padang Bai. Candi Dasa was once a sleepy fishing village and is now a sleepy tourist town that bears no resemblance to those further south. Along the strip that includes the villages of Buitan, Sengkidu and Candi Dasa there's a noticeable absence of street vendors but respectable tourist facilities including local and international restaurants and a few iconic bars. The three islands of Nusa Penida, Nusa Ceningan and Nusa Lembongan off the east coast are slowly opening up to tourism.

Above: While Gianyar is the administrative capital, few visitors stay here long as the nearby beaches of black sands are not appealing. Its three-storey market is home to the famous spit-roasted suckling pig called 'babi guling'.

Right: The foothills of the volcanic mountains in the northeast support rich soils which are ideal for growing crops such as chillies. Mount Agung towers in the background and the village of Sidemen is surrounded by rice terraces. Farmers tending their crops are commonly seen along this road.

Left: Misguided development over the past few decades has lead to the deterioration of the beaches and reef of Candi Dasa, so that most visitors are content to relax around pools at hotels such as Rama Candidasa Resort and Spa or to go on diving and snorkelling excursions out to sea. A reasonable wave rolls in here to attract the attention of boardriders.

Below left: The main attraction in Tirtagangga to the north of Candi Dasa is the beautiful Water Palace which looks old but in fact only dates back to 1947. It was built by Anak Agung Anglurah, the last Raja of Karangasem. This peaceful retreat of fountains, ponds and terraces interspersed with manicured gardens makes for a relaxing day away from the beach. Visitors may swim in two pools here and there are tranquil and shaded places from which to take in the ambiance.

Chapter 3: Northern Bali

The northern coastline borders the Bali Sea. Few tourists venture northwards but those who do are attracted here because it is less crowded and more peaceful than most other resort areas. Access is generally by road from the south and across the mountainous interior. Even fewer tourists venture along the northeast coast with most arriving via two main roads – one passing through Kintamani and the other via Bedugul. Lava flows in the northeast restrict agricultural activity but there are some fine examples of sculptured rice terraces in other parts of the north.

Singaraja

Singaraja (which means 'lion king') is the main centre and Bali's second largest city. The port was once Bali's most important and a strategic location for the Dutch who occupied the city and traded from here. There is very little evidence of the port these days or of the colonial architecture which dates back to the Dutch administration that extended from 1849 to 1953.

This page: While most visitors pass through Singaraja on their way to the beaches around Lovina to the west, there are several places of interest in the city. Gedong Kirtya, instantly recognized by its colourful wooden gate, is an old library and museum dedicated to preserving documents on old paper called 'lontar'. Another dominant monument in the city centre is the Singambaraja or 'winged lion' which is the city symbol and strategically located in the middle of the road in front of the Governor's Office.

Above: Down by the former harbour of Buleleng, the striking Yudha Mandalatama Independence Statue features a local freedom fighter who was killed in the war against the Dutch in 1945.

Above right: Singaraja's ethnic mix of Balinese, Chinese and Muslims is reflected in its various places of worship. The Chinese Buddhist temple or 'klenteng' called Ling Gwan Kiong is one of several places of worship for the Chinese community. It was built in 1873 and is located in Buleleng in front of the statue.

Right: One of Bali's most spectacular waterfalls cascades from its forested surroundings in Gitgit just to the south of Singaraja. It is accessed via a 500 m (1,640 ft) walk through 'padi' fields and the inevitable avenue of souvenir stalls. Water cascades 40 m (131 ft) into a deep but cool pool which is suitable for a refreshing dip.

Lovina

Lovina encompasses six villages of which Kalibukbuk is considered the centre. It has an eight kilometre (five-mile) long stretch of mostly black sands. Many villagers depend upon fishing for an income and many traditional fishing boats or *jukung* line the beaches. Some fishermen now operate as dolphin-watching guides hiring out their boats each morning to those who want to witness this natural spectacle.

Nothing ever gets too busy here and the lifestyle is relaxed with a subdued nightlife. Many guests are content to laze around resort pools such as that at the Sunari Villas and Spa Resort.

This page: Many of the locals fish from traditional outrigger canoes; the same kind that are also used to take tourists on dolphin-watching trips.

Opposite top: A long stretch of tourist facilities, including shops, restaurants, cafés and bars, lines the main road through Lovina.

Opposite below: While many beaches in the north have black sands, they are always picturesque from the brightly coloured fishing boats moored there.

These pages: In Bajar near Lovina, the Brahma Vihara Arama, built in 1970, is Bali's only Buddhist monastery. At the rear of the main temple is a scaled replica of the famous Borobudur Temple in Java (above), providing an alternative to those who can't visit the original ninth century temple in Magelang, Java.

Above: Hot spring pools are nearby at Banjar Tega (Air Panas Banjar). Three pools with eight naga (mythical serpents) heads that spout warm spring water are popular for bathing with both locals and tourists.

The Northwest

Bali's northwest is the least populated part of the island and is dominated by an expansive national park and sparsely located settlements that grip the coastline. The most remote town is Gilimanuk which is the departure port for ferries heading westward to the adjoining island of Java.

West Bali National Park (Taman Nasional Bali Barat) at 19 km² (73 sq miles) is an important feature of the northwestern landscape. Several peaks over 300 m (1,000 ft) are located in the park and adjoining forest. A road circumnavigates three sides of the park's perimeter with a few walking trails heading off from the main road.

Above: While rainforest covers many parts of the West Bali National Park – the main road on the north coast traverses several dense stands – other parts of the park resemble African savannah. These are much drier and lower with much more open vegetation than the rainforest.

Left: Various habitats are protected in the park the main ones of which are coral reefs, rainforests (called monsoon forests on Bali), savannah and mangroves. One of the most accessible stands of mangroves can be seen at Labuhan Lalang, which is the departure point for ferries to Deer Island (Pulau Menjangan). There is a national park office here and it's possible to see the mountainous peaks of Java on the horizon.

Left: Visitors mostly only pass through the port of Gilimanuk, Bali's westernmost town. It faces the Bali Strait and car and passenger ferries regularly make the 2.4-km (1½-mile) crossing to Ketapang on Java. The National Park headquarters are also located here.

Below: Pura Agung Pulaki, just west of Pemuteran on the north coast, is fascinating in that the cliff face temple is overrun by a troop of Long-tailed Macaques who are more water- than land-based: they love to swim and feed in the coastal waters.

West to Northwest

Bali's most popular beaches peter out just north of Seminyak after which the coastline heads northwest from the famous temple of Tanah Lot to Gilimanuk about 100 km (62 miles) away in the island's far west. This is one of Bali's most sparsely populated areas criss-crossed by wild streams and lined with rugged beaches. Being so close to Java also means that tourists may see more mosques here than temples.

Above: The majority of tourists who venture here are on their way to Java via the ferry crossing at Gilimanuk. Others come to surf – one of the most famous breaks is at Medewi, a village lined with colourful fishing boats.

Right: Many wild rivers flow from the mountainous interior to the sea on Bali's west coast.

Above: Another coastal temple also has impressive views: Pura Rambut Siwi, just west of Medewi, sits high above the black sand beach surrounded by 'padi' fields and coconut plantations.

Top and above: Tanah Lot is possibly the most visited site on Bali and, with its dramatic island location, black sand beaches, crashing waves and sunset views, it's easy to see why many flock here especially at day's end. During religious festivals it gets even more crowded. The temple dates back to the 16th century and while it's possible to visit it at low tide, there are also good views from the mainland.

   Arguably the best view of the temple is from the adjoining Pan Pacific Nirwana Bali Resort with its elevated southerly position. The resort incorporates the Nirwana Bali Golf Club designed by Greg Norman. This is one of Norman's most picturesque courses with the legendary 169 m (185 yard), par 3, seventh hole gripping the coastline and leading golfers to tee off across the bay onto the green perched near the temple.

Chapter 4: The Interior of Bali

Much of the interior of Bali is mountainous made up of the great peaks of Agung, Abang, Batur and Batukaru. Away from the beaches and coastal lowlands, these volcanic peaks rise high above the landscape and can be seen from most parts of the island as well as from neighbouring Lombok.

Below: The rich volcanic soil on the lower slopes of Mount Agung is ideal for growing crops such as rice, chillies, vegetables and fruit. Many of these can be seen growing in Sidemen on the road from Klungkung to Besakih.

Left: Bali's highest peak, Mount Agung, is an active volcano that last erupted in 1964. Mount Batur (1,717 m/ 5,633 ft) experienced shallow earthquakes as recently as 2009. Batur is now protected as a UNESCO Geopark.

Above and left: Bali's highest peak is revered by Balinese as it is considered a spiritual and sacred mountain. Its holiest temple, Besakih, is located in the foothills. There are two paths to the peak but there are certain times when they cannot be climbed for religious reasons (for example, during the Bhatar Turun Kabeh festival in March or April the temple and ascent are normally off-limits). Tourists set off around midnight to capture the sunrise at 7 a.m.

All mountains are Hindu holy mountains since they are the source of water and the home of deities. Besakih is known as the 'mother temple'. It has 22 separate temples and the central one of Pura Penataran Agung is Bali's largest. Only those praying or making offerings are allowed to enter these temples although walkways between the temples are accessible to visitors.

Left and right: Tourists continue from Besakih northwest to Kedisan to take in the picturesque views of Lake Batur (left) sandwiched between Mount Abang and Mount Batur. There are several viewing spots at Kedisan, Penelokan, Batur and Kintamani. These towns are on the crater rim looking down into the caldera. Trekkers head off early in the morning to climb to Mount Batur's summit and watch the sunrise.

Lakes Tamblingan (right) and Buyen are two other scenic lakes to the northwest of Bedugul on a side road through to the northwest coast.

Left: Another approach to the interior heads north from Bangli towards Bedugul, Lake Bratan and on to Singaraja on the north coast. Temples are situated around the foreshores of the lakes in the region with Pura Ulun Danu (pictured) on Lake Bratan being one of Bali's most revered, ornate and photographed. Bedugul Botanic Gardens (Keban Raya Eka Karya) is a popular tourist site as is the daily market. The gardens are a branch of the famous Bogor Botanic Gardens in Java.

Chapter 5: Lombok and the Gili Islands

There are several islands off the coast of Bali, the largest of which are Nusa Penida to the southeast and Lombok to the east. Lombok is an island in Indonesia's Nusa Tenggara Province that forms part of the Lesser Sunda Islands. The Lombok Strait separates the island from Bali to the west.

Visitors are attracted to Lombok for its cultural features, the variety of its landscapes and because it is less commercialized than Bali's main tourist areas. Others travel here to climb its tallest peak, Mount Rinjani (3,726 m, 12,224 ft), visible from many parts of the island.

Above: *Lombok differs from Bali in that the Sasak people (85% of Lombok's 3.2 million people) who live here are mostly Muslims so mosques are a more common sight than temples. The mosque in Labuapi Village south of the main conurbation of Mataram-Cakranegara is colourful and ornate while many others appear to be permanently under repair.*

Right: *Sasak architecture is unique with the 'lumbung' or rice barn being the traditional way of storing rice between harvests. This thatched barn built on stilts is mainly found in the south and east – the most accessible for tourists are in Sade village near Kuta.*

Above: While there are pockets of tourism concentred on the beaches of Senggigi and Kuta (not to be confused with Bali's Kuta), most inhabitants of Lombok are farmers whose main crop is rice grown in the rich volcanic soil. Other crops include soyabeans, coffee, tobacco, corn, cotton, peanuts and vanilla.

Right: Woven textiles have always been an important part of Sasak culture. Sukarara is the most commercial weaving village on the island where visitors can both see 'ikat' and 'songket' cloth being woven and purchase items. While natural dyes were once used, industrial dyes are more common these days.

Above: Resort development extends from just south of Senggigi northwards where some of the beaches are covered in black sand due to their volcanic origins. Colourful and traditional wooden fishing boats (called 'jukung') line some of the beaches. These are approximately 5 m (16½ ft) long and use a single main cloth sail to project them across the water. Bamboo outriggers on both sides provide stability in the open sea.

Right: The beaches at Senggigi are the main reason people come to Lombok. While nothing like the density of resorts and intensity of life on Bali exists on Lombok, laid-back Senggigi is the closest thing on Lombok to resort living. Golden sandy beaches and shallow turquoise waters within fringing reefs appeal to those seeking the magical combination of accommodation in beachside resorts, smart restaurants and a tranquil bar scene.

This page: It is worth visiting the Hindu temple, Pura Batu Bolong, as it affords one of the best coastal views of Senggigi and some spectacular sunsets. Located one kilometre (two-thirds of a mile) south of Senggigi, the black stone temple has been built on a rocky promontory and is oriented towards Bali's most sacred mountain – Mount Agung – across the Lombok Strait.

The road extends 25 km (16 miles) northwards to the small port of Bangsal, which is the departure point for boats heading to the Gili Islands. There isn't much tourism infrastructure here and it is mostly a transit point although the road continues northwards and onwards, basically circumnavigating the island.

The South

Southern Lombok is much drier and flatter than the island's north and water shortage and crop failure aren't uncommon. Apart from the restrained tourism development along Kuta Beach in the far south, farming is the principal activity here and on the central plain beneath Mount Rinjani.

Right: The small fishing village of Gerupak in the far southeast of Lombok is a popular departure point for surfers who head offshore to the reef breaks.

Below: Kuta Beach is laid-back and leisurely. The luxurious Novotel Lombok Resort is the only resort of substance along a picturesque beach with a coral reef situated just off shore.

Left: Nearby, Sade is a Sasak village known, along with those of Pringgasela and Sukarara, for its traditional textiles. Villagers here weave 'ikat' or 'songket' cloth often with distinctive patterns that have been handed down from mother to daughter.

Below: Just north of Kuta in the small town of Sengkol the Thursday market isn't to be missed. This open-air roadside market starts early and by midday most traders have sold their vegetables and produce and returned home. The road is almost impassable as traders and shoppers jostle to buy goods ranging from sweetcorn to locally-grown tobacco. The barber does a flourishing trade under a rudimentary shelter and horse-drawn carts transport people and produce to surrounding villages.

Above: While similar in name, Kuta Lombok and Kuta Bali are poles apart in what they offer tourists. Kuta Lombok (or Pantai Putri Nyale) is relaxed and while the infrastructure caters more to backpackers, there are some smart but small resorts, cafés and bars along the long sweeping bay. Offshore reefs are popular with young surfers using Kuta as their base for riding the breakers at Selong Blanak, Tanjung Aan Beach and Awang Bay.

Mataram and Beyond

Mataram on the west coast is the provincial capital and largest city. There is little distinction between the river mouth settlement of Ampenan, Mataram, Sweta and Cakranegara as they form one continuous urban sprawl housing a population of over 500,000. Mount Rinjani towers over the northern part of the island. At 3,726 m (12,221 feet), it is Indonesia's second largest volcano with a 6 by 8.5-km (3½ by 5-mile) caldera. Climbers depart from either Senaru (northern approach) or Sembalun (eastern approach). Joining an organized group is recommended as Rinjani is an active volcano.

Above: Climbing Mount Rinjani to see the lake in the caldera is the most rewarding of all the mountain climbs on both Bali and Lombok.

Above right: The Lombok landscape is dotted with mosques many of which appear to be in various stages of construction or repair.

Right: The old port of Ampenan on the Jangkok River was once a maze of old shophouses and warehouses operated by the original Chinese and Arab traders. Many of these buildings are now run down but fishermen moor their boats along the riverbanks.

Above: Just to the east is the holy shrine of Pura Lingsar built around 1714. Interestingly, it is a focus of worship for both Hindus and Muslims. This large complex is also popular for fishing with several ponds located in the outer courtyards.

Above left: Cakranegara (or 'Cakra' and pronounced 'Changra') was the capital in the 18th century when Balinese influence on Lombok was at its peak. It is now the commercial centre and good for shopping.

Left: Lombok's handmade pottery is quite distinctive in that the pieces are burnished to give the surface a bright sheen before being fired in the ground using coconut husks. Patterns on the surface are hand-etched. The three pottery villages of Banyumulek, Penujak and Masbagik are the best places to see the work.

Gili Islands

There are several smaller islands surrounding Lombok, known locally as 'gili'. The Gili Islands just off Lombok's northwest coastline are already established as a tourist destination in their own right. There are three islands in the group – Trawangan, Meno and Air – with Trawangan being the largest. Peak tourism months are July, August, December and January. Various boats service the islands from Bangsal on Lombok and Padang Bai on Bali. Fast boats make the journey from Bangsal to Trawangan in less than 30 minutes. Boats also provide a service between the islands.

Above right: Life on all three of the Gili Islands moves at a decidedly unhurried pace. The only forms of transport are bicycles or horse-drawn carts called 'cidomo'. All islands are low, flat and small enough to walk around: it takes just two hours to walk round Trawangan.

Right and opposite page: The Gilis have a reputation as a tropical paradise with most of the chalet accommodation located close to the water's edge. Visitors travel here for the relaxed beach lifestyle, surfing, diving, sunset-gazing, snorkelling and the après-sun party atmosphere especially on Trawangan.

There are many diving schools. Young budget travellers are especially attracted here although more sophisticated accommodation, bars and restaurants are appearing in order to cater to a wider travelling audience. While the locals are mostly Muslim, they are tolerant of the ways of tourists.

Getting About

There are international airports on both Bali and Lombok. Bali's upgraded Ngurah Rai Airport is located on the narrowest strip of land near Jimbaran on the southern part of the island and protrudes westward into the Bali Strait. Lombok's new Bandara International Airport is located southwest of Mataram.

Bali is Indonesia's third busiest airport after those of the capital, Jakarta, and Surabaya. International flights arrive from many parts of the world along with domestic services from several destinations in Indonesia. By contrast, Lombok is Indonesia's 15th busiest airport. While Bali's airport is officially known and coded in the airline industry as 'DPS', for Denpasar, the actual airport is some distance from Bali's principal city.

Above: Many locals use small mini vans, called 'bemos', to travel generally short distances around both Bali and Lombok.

Below: Access to the Gili Islands is by sea with boats such as this one providing a fast service to Bali and back.

Most visitors will be transferred to their accommodation by air-conditioned coaches, mini-vans or limousines while those on a budget may use the services of local open-sided vehicles. To get around Bali, there are modern air-conditioned taxis or cars available to rent from one of many travel agents.

Other short-distance forms of transportation include motorbikes, bicycles and in some cases, horse-drawn carts or *cidomo,* especially on Lombok. Surfers ride modified motorbikes with a side support for their boards. Ferries and boats, including local *perahu* or *jukung* with bamboo outriggers, are available to charter or are used for dive and snorkelling trips to offshore reefs.

Above: Push bikes are a popular means of getting around for tourists, especially on the Gili Islands where they are the main form of transport after walking.

Left: There is no mechanized transportation on the Gili Islands – many visitors choose to use the novel services of a horse and cart or 'cidomo' to move around.

Resources

Useful websites

Bumbu Bali Restaurant and Cooking School:
www.balifoods.com

Explorer Tourism Network: www.etn.my

Nexplorer Representatives & Travel Services:
www.n-explorer.com

Sarinbuana Eco Lodge: www.baliecolodge.com

Waterbom Bali: www.waterbom-bali.com

Accor Hotels: www.accorhotels.com

Alila Ubud: www.alilahotels.com

Ayana Resort and Spa Bali: www.ayanaresort.com

Bali For Kids: www.baliforkids.com

Bali Hotels Association: www.balihotelsassociation.com

Bali Zoo: www.bali-zoo.com

Bumbu Bali Restaurant and Cooking School: www.balifoods.
com

Nirwana Bali Golf Club: www.nirwanabaligolf.com

Pan Pacific Nirwana Bali: www.panpacific.com

Rama Candidasa Resort and Spa: www.ramacandidasahotel.
com

Sarinbuana Eco-Lodge: www.baliecolodge.com

The Chedi Club Ubud: www.ghmhotels.com

UNESCO World Heritage Sites: www.whc.unesco.org

World Wide Fund (WWF) Indonesia: www.wwf.or.id

Airlines

Garuda: www.garuda-indonesia.com

Indonesia Air: www.indonesia-air.com

AirAsia: www.airasia.com

Lion Air: www.lionair.co.id

Merpati Nusantara Airlines: www.merpati.co.id

References

Sochaczewski, P. S. 2012. *An Inordinate Fondness for Beetles*. Editions Didier Millet.

Von Holzen, H. 2004. *Bali Unveiled: The Secrets of Balinese Cuisine*. Marshall Cavendish.

Acknowledgements

The author would like to thank his diligent and knowledgeable guides and drivers, Lenong and Gede, on Bali and Lombok. Erwin Nalaprana, Herman Lim, Abubakar, Heinz von Holzen and Linda vant Hoff are also thanked for their kind assistance and keen insight into the islands.

The publishers and the author would like to express special thanks to Ken Scriven for his advice and support during the preparation of this book.

About the Author

David Bowden is a freelance photojournalist based in Malaysia specializing in travel and the environment. While Australian, he's been in Asia for longer than he can remember and returns to his home country as a tourist. When he's not travelling the world, he enjoys relaxing with his equally adventurous wife, Maria and daughter, Zoe. He is also the author of other books in this series, *Enchanting Borneo*, *Singapore*, *Malaysia* and *Langkawi*.

Index

First published in the United Kingdom in 2013 by John Beaufoy Publishing,
11 Blenheim Court, 316 Woodstock Road, Oxford OX2 7NS, England
www.johnbeaufoy.com

ISBN 978-1-906780-93-7

Designed by Glyn Bridgewater
Cartography by William Smuts
Project management by Rosemary Wilkinson

Printed and bound in in Malaysia by Tien Wah Press (Pte) Ltd.

All photos by David Bowden except for: Accor Hotels (p35, p70 bottom); Shutterstock/Laurent Ruelle
(p23 bottom right); Visit Indonesia (p72 centre left).

Cover captions and credits
Back cover (left to right): *Orchids grow all over the island,* © David Bowden; *Sports and leisure at Geger beach,*
Bali, © David Bowden; *A Balinese painter at Ubud,* © David Bowden; *One of the villa pools at the Novotel
Lombok,* © David Bowden. Front cover (top, left to right): *Coral reefs await divers,* © David Bowden; *A traditional
Balinese dancer at the Ubud Dance Festival,* © Shutterstock.com/jaja; *Rice terraces near Ubud,* © David Bowden;
The endemic Jalak Bali or Rothschild's Myna, © Shutterstock/Laurent Ruelle. Front cover (centre): *Inside Batur
volcano, Bali,* © Shutterstock.com/saiko3p. Front cover (bottom): *Pura Tanah Lot at sunset, Bali,*
© Shutterstock.com/Elena Anisimova.